STOICISM QUOTES ON MONEY & WEALTH

STOICISM QUOTES ON MONEY & WEALTH

Timeless Financial Wisdom from the Greatest Stoic Minds

NICK BENAS, USMC &
KORTNEY YASENKA, LCMHC

Hatherleigh Press, Ltd.
62545 State Highway 10
Hobart, NY 13788, USA
hatherleighpress.com

hatherleigh

STOICISM QUOTES ON MONEY & WEALTH

Library of Congress Cataloging-in-Publication Data is available.

ISBN: 978-1-961293-68-7

Cover by Carolyn Casper

Printed in the United States

The authorized representative in the EU for product safety and compliance is Catarina Astrom, Blästorpsvägen 14, 276 35 Borrby, Sweden. info@hatherleighpress.com

10 9 8 7 6 5 4 3 2 1

To Mario Lupone

Contents

Introduction

WITHIN THESE PAGES LIE the enduring words of the greatest Greek and Roman Stoics—great perspectives on how to live in accordance with wealth.The Stoics never offered "get rich quick" schemes or formulas on how to amass great fortunes.They offered relationship(s) and an indifference to the money, resources and the power that came along with wealth. Zeno of Citium, the founder of Stoicism, knew both sides of fortune. Born into a merchant family, he once had it all. Then he lost everything when a shipment of murex snails...the source of Tyrian deep reddish-purple dye for the elite...sank into the Mediterranean. His fortune went under. His philosophy rose up.This book isn't about getting rich quick. It's about wealth the way the Stoics saw it. No formulas. No hacks. Just timeless wisdom. As Marcus Aurelius said, "Acquire the habit of attending carefully to what is being said by another, and of entering, so far as possible, into the mind of the speaker."

Some Stoics lived with riches. Others were enslaved with nothing but a tunic on their backs. The common thread? They understood that wealth is never about what you own. It's about how you think, how you live, and what you can endure.

Today, we live in a world where wealth is measured in likes, followers, and numbers on a screen. The chase is endless. The next deal, the next raise, the next shiny thing, it all promises fulfillment but rarely delivers. And when the bottom falls out, when the market dips, the job is lost, or the house feels heavier than a home, we're left asking: Was it worth it?

This is where Stoicism still speaks, loud and clear. The Stoics remind us that wealth is never the enemy. The trap is believing it defines us. Seneca put it bluntly: riches are indifferent. What matters is our relationship to them. Do we own our money, or does it own us?

Stoicism cuts through the noise and brings us back to center. It teaches us to hold money like a tool, not a trophy. To use it for freedom, generosity, and purpose, not ego, status, or fear. Marcus Aurelius ruled the largest empire in the world, yet he wrote more about humility than power. That's no accident. He knew true abundance wasn't outside of him, it was inside, in how he lived and led.

And here's the truth: financial storms will come. Markets crash, businesses fold, fortunes fade. But if we build our foundation on Stoic principles, discipline, perspective, resilience, no storm can strip us of what matters most. Wealth becomes a resource, not a ruler.

Why does Stoicism still matter in wealth? Because it reminds us that prosperity isn't about what we accumulate, it's about who we become. And when we learn to measure wealth by integrity, wisdom, and freedom, we discover a kind of fortune that never depreciates.

I

FORTUNE & PHILOSOPHY

"Wealth consists not in having great possessions, but in having few wants."

—Epictetus

LIFE HAS A WAY of teaching us just how fragile fortune really is. One day we're riding high, the next it's gone...markets crash, businesses fold, opportunities slip through our hands. Wealth can disappear in an instant, and when it does, we're left staring at the same question: Who are we without it?

That's where philosophy steps in. The Stoics saw money for what it is, useful, yes, but never ultimate. They understood that possessions don't define character, and losing them doesn't strip us of dignity. What matters isn't the rise and fall of our bank account, but how we respond when things don't go our way.

The Stoic approach to wealth is disarmingly simple: money is indifferent. It's neither good nor bad until we give it power. When we let it control us, we lose freedom. When we treat it as a tool, something to build, to share, to live with purpose—we stay grounded.

The first rule is clear: never let fortune own you. Hold it loosely. Respect its role, but don't mistake it for peace, happiness, or meaning. Because real security doesn't come from what we store up, it comes from cultivating wisdom, discipline, and resilience.

The Stoics remind us: fortune is fickle, but philosophy endures. And when life strips us of everything external, we discover the one form of wealth no one can ever take, our ability to choose how we live, respond, and grow.

"No person has the power to have everything they want but is in their power not to want what they don't have, and to cheerfully put to good use what they do have."

—SENECA

"When you arise in the morning, think of what a precious privilege it is to be alive, to breathe, to think, to enjoy, to love."

—MARCUS AURELIUS

"The Lamp of wisdom shines brightest when lit by the flame of self-awareness."

—MUSONIUS RUFUS

"It is in times of security that the spirit should be preparing itself for difficult times; while fortune is bestowing favors on it, then is the time for it be strengthened against her rebuffs."

—SENECA

"Objective judgment, now, at this very moment. Unselfish action, now, at this very moment. Willing acceptance, now at this very moment, of all external events. That's all you need."

—MARCUS AURELIUS

"As far as I am concerned, I know that I have lost not wealth but distractions."

—SENECA

"Never value anything as profitable that compels you to break your promise, to lose your self-respect, to hate any man, to suspect, to curse, to act the hypocrite, to desire anything that needs walls and curtains."

—MARCUS AURELIUS

"The essence of good and evil consists in the condition of our character. And externals are the means by which our character finds its particular good and evil."

—EPICTETUS

"All cruelty springs from weakness."

SENECA

"Never let the future disturb you. You will meet it, if you have to, with the same weapons of reason which today arm you against the present."

—MARCUS AURELIUS

"Under no circumstances ever say 'I lost it.'"

—EPICTETUS

"Virtue alone affords everlasting and peace-giving joy; even if some obstacles arise, it is but like an intervening cloud, which floats beneath the sun but never prevails against it."

—SENECA

"If it is not right, do not do it: if it is not true, do not say it. For let your impulse be in your own power."

—MARCUS AURELIUS

"Death is necessary and cannot be avoided. I mean, where am I going to go to get away from it?"

—EPICTETUS

"So I look for the best and am prepared for the opposite."

—SENECA

"It's silly to try and escape other people's faults. They are inescapable. Just try to escape your own."

—MARCUS AURELIUS

"One thing alone can bring us peace, an agreement to treat one another with kindness."

—SENECA

"What does Socrates Say? 'One person likes tending to his farm, another to his horse; I like to daily monitor my self improvement.'"

—EPICTETUS

"The important thing about a problem is not its solution, but the strength we gain in finding the solution."

—SENECA

"Whenever you are about to find fault with someone. Ask yourself the following question: what fault of mine most nearly resembles the one I am about to criticize?"

—MARCUS AURELIUS

"We are more often frightened than hurt; and we suffer more from imagination than from reality."

—SENECA

"You live as if you were destined to live forever, no thought of your frailty ever enters your head, of how much time has already gone by you take no heed. You squander time as if you drew from a full and abundant supply, though all the while that day which you bestow on some person or things is perhaps your last."

—SENECA

"Every soul is deprived of the truth against its will."

—PLATO

"There is nothing dangerous in a man's having as much power as he likes if he takes the view that he has power to do only what it is his duty to do."

—SENECA

"If you have been placed in a position above others, are you automatically going to behave like a despot? Remember who you are and whom you govern, they are kinsmen, brothers by nature, fellow descendants of Zeus."

—EPICTETUS

"You can pass your life in an equable flow of happiness if you can follow the right way and think and act in the right way."

—MARCUS AURELIUS

"You need not look about for the reward of a just deed; a just deed in itself offers a still greater return."

—SENECA

"Confine yourself to the present."

—MARCUS AURELIUS

"When a man has said: 'I have lived! every morning he arises he receives a bonus.'"

—SENECA

"You could leave life right now. Let that determine what you do and say and think."

—MARCUS AURELIUS

II

REAL RICHES

"It is not the man who has too little, but the man who craves more, that is poor."

—Seneca

THE STOICS REMIND US that wealth is not measured in our coins but in character. You can have a palatial home filled with treasure, a ledger filled with large numbers and still be bankrupt in spirit. Time, virtue, and peace of mind, these are the riches that outlast any fortune.

Marcus Aurelius ruled the largest empire on earth, yet his private writings echo with reminders: stay humble, remember death, hold close what matters most. He knew emperors rot in the ground the same as beggars.

What makes you rich is not what sits in your bitcoin wallet but what no one can take away: your integrity, your discipline, and your ability to be content right now.

The Stoics saw real riches as a radical shift away from anything that can be gained or lost. Thinkers like Seneca argued that wealth often enslaves rather than frees us; the more we have, the more we fear losing it. Epictetus took this further, teaching that true wealth lies in wanting less, not having more, since desire itself is what creates a sense of poverty. For Marcus Aurelius, real riches were rooted in the inner life: a disciplined mind, moral clarity, and the ability to accept reality without resistance.

In this sense, Stoic wealth is not passive contentment but an active mastery of perception. It's about choosing to value what is within your control (your thoughts, choices, and character) and releasing your attachment to everything else. When you no longer depend on external things for your sense of worth or stability, you become, in Stoic terms, truly "rich," because nothing essential can be taken from you.

"Health is the soul that animates all the enjoyments of life, which fade and are tasteless without it."

—SENECA

"You become what you give your attention to…If you yourself don't choose what thoughts and images you expose yourself to, someone else will."

—EPICTETUS

"He has the most who is content with the least."

—DIOGENES

"Moreover; friendship is not only an indispensable, but also a beautiful or noble thing: for we commend those who love their friends, and to have many friends is thought to be a noble thing; and some even think that a good man is the same as a friend."

—ARISTOTLE

"The parched earth loves the rain, And the high heaven, with moisture laden, loves Earthwards to fall."

—EURIPIDES

"Opposites fit together,' and 'Out of discordant elements comes the fairest harmony,' and 'It is by battle that all things come into the world.'"

—HERACLITUS

"Like desires like."

—EMPEDOCLES

"Love seems to be implanted by nature in the parent towards the offspring, and in the offspring towards the parent, not only among men, but also among birds and most animals; and in those of the same race towards one another, among men especially, for which reason we commend those who love their fellow men. And when one travels one may see how man is always akin to and dear to man."

—ARISTOTLE

"Very little is needed to make a happy life; it is all within yourself, in your way of thinking."

—MARCUS AURELIUS

"This is why we need to envisage every possibility and to strengthen the spirit of the deal with the things which may conceivably come about."

—SENECA

"Again, it seems that friendship is the bond that holds states together, and that lawgivers are even more eager to secure it than justice. For concord bears a certain resemblance to friendship, and that they especially wish to retain, and dissension that they wish to banish as an enemy. If citizens be friends, they have no need of justice, but they be just, they need friendship or love also; indeed, the completest realization of justice seems to be the realization of friendship or love also."

—ARISTOTLE

"If a man is mistaken, instruct him kindly and show him his error."

—MARCUS AURELIUS

"Crimes often return to their teacher."

—SENECA

"You will earn the respect of all men if you begin by earning the respect of yourself."

—MUSONIUS RUFUS

"I begin to speak only when I'm certain what I'll say isn't better left unsaid."

—CATO THE YOUNGER

"Let us take pleasure in what we have received and make no comparison; no man will ever be happy if tortured by the greater happiness of another."

—SENECA

"A room without books is like a body without a soul."

—CICERO

"If you really want to escape the things that harass you, what you're needing is not to be in a different place but to be a different person."

—SENECA

"It has always been a rule that the weak should be subject to the strong; and besides, we consider that we are worthy of our power. Up till the present moment, you too, used to think that we were; but now, after calculating your own interest, you are beginning to talk in terms of right and wrong. Considerations of this kind have never yet turned people aside from the opportunities of aggrandizement offered by superior strength."

—THUCYDIDES

"We have two ears and one mouth, so we should listen more than we say."

—ZENO OF CITIUM, AS QUOTED BY DIOGENES LAËRTIUS

"Since it happens that the human being is not soul alone, nor body alone, but a kind of synthesis of the two, the person in training must take care of both, the better part, the soul, more zealously; as is fitting, but also of the other, if he shall not be found lacking in any part that constitutes man."

—MUSONIUS RUFUS

"We should eat to live, not live to eat."

—SOCRATES

"Gratitude is not only the greatest of virtues, but the parent of all others."

—CICERO

"Let food be thy medicine and medicine be thy food."

—HIPPOCRATES

"We can easily forgive a child who is afraid of the dark; the real tragedy of life is when men are afraid of the light."

—PLATO

"The best seasoning for food is hunger."

—SOCRATES

"It is circumstances (difficulties) which show what men are. Therefore when a difficulty falls upon you, remember that God, like a trainer of wrestlers, has matched you with a rough young man. For what purpose? you may say. Why, that you may become an Olympic conqueror; but it is not accomplished without sweat. In my opinion no man has had a more profitable difficulty than you have had, if you choose to make use of it as an athlete would deal with a young antagonist."

—EPICTETUS

"He who eats with most pleasure is he who least requires sauce."

—SENECA

"The body is a community made up of its innumerable cells or inhabitants."

—MARCUS AURELIUS

"People walk in wickedness all their lives or, at any rate, for the greater part of it. If they ever attain to virtue, it is late and at the very sunset of their days"

—CLEANTHES

"Happiness is a good flow of life."

—ZENO OF CITIUM

III

DESIRE & DISCIPLINE

"Wealth is the slave of a wise man and the master of a fool."

—Seneca

DESIRE IS A FIRE. If you don't control it, it consumes you. The Stoics trained themselves to want less, so they could live more. They practiced "negative visualization": imagine losing what you have, and suddenly you see how little you actually need.

Modern life runs on advertising designed to inflame desire…more, newer, faster, and shinier. The Stoics knew this trap centuries ago. Epictetus, born a slave, taught that freedom begins when you cut the chains of craving.

The true discipline of desire isn't about denying yourself everything. It's about knowing the difference between needs and wants and being strong enough to stop where enough is enough.

In Stoicism, the discipline of desire teaches you to align your wants with what is truly within your control. Rather than chasing external outcomes, such as wealth, status, or the approval of others, Stoic thinkers like Epictetus and Marcus Aurelius emphasized training yourself to desire only what nature and circumstance would allow. When you focus your desires on your own character, choices, and responses, you free yourself from constant disappointment and frustration.

The discipline of desire encourages acceptance of events as they unfold and cultivates gratitude for the present moment. By reshaping what you want, you gain inner stability and peace—your fulfillment no longer depends on things outside your control

"Settle on the type of person you want to be and stick to it, whether alone or in company."

—EPICTETUS

"The body ought to be compact, and to show no irregularity either in motion or attitude. For what the mind shows in the face by maintaining in it the expression of intelligence and propriety, that ought to be required also in the whole body. But all of these things should be observed without affection."

—MARCUS AURELIUS

"The unexamined life is not worth living."

—SENECA

"If you like doing something, do it regularly; if you don't like doing something, make a habit of doing something different. The same goes for moral inclinations."

—EPICTETUS

"The best way to keep good acts in memory is to refresh them with the new."

—CATO THE YOUNGER

"I would much rather have men ask why I have no statue than why I have one."

—CATO THE YOUNGER

"Cling, therefore, to this sound and wholesome plan of life; indulge the body just so far as suffices for good health... Your food should appease your hunger, your drink quenches your thirst, your clothing keep out of the cold, your house be a protection against inclement weather, it makes no difference whether it is built of turf or variegated marble imported from another country."

—SENECA

"Man conquers the world by conquering himself."

—ZENO OF CITIUM

"Adopt new habits yourself: consolidate your principles by putting them into practice."

—EPICTETUS

"Most powerful is he who has himself in his own power."

—SENECA

"Concentrate every minute on doing what's in front of you with precise and genuine seriousness, tenderly, willingly, with justice. And on freeing yourself from all other distractions."

—MARCUS AURELIUS

"No great thing is created suddenly, any more than a bunch of grapes or a fig."

—EPICTETUS

"For obviously the philosopher's body should be well prepared for physical activity, because often the virtues make use of this as a necessary instrument for the affairs of life."

—MUSONIUS RUFUS

"A man thus grounded must, whether he wills or not, necessarily be attended by constant cheerfulness and a joy that is deep and issues from deep within, since he finds delight in his own resources, and desires no joys greater than his inner joys."

—SENECA

"If you are careless and lazy now and keep putting things off and always deferring the day after which you will attend to yourself, you will not notice that you are making no progress but you will live and dies as someone quite ordinary."

—EPICTETUS

"No man has the right to be amateur in the matter of physical training. It is a shame for a man to grow old without seeing the beauty and strength of which his body is capable."

—SOCRATES

"Just as you must not force fertile farmland, as uninterrupted productivity will soon exhaust it, so constant effort will sap our mental vigor, while a short period of rest and relaxation will restore our powers."

—SENECA

"Flee laziness, because the indolence of the soul is the decay of the body."

—CATO THE YOUNGER

"The object of your love is mortal; and not one of your possessions."

—EPICTETUS

"Others have been in poor health from over indulgence and high living, before exile has provided strength, forcing them to live a more vigorous life."

—MUSONIUS RUFUS

"Difficulties strengthen the mind, as labor does the body."

—SENECA

"If we try to adapt our mind to the regular sequence of changes and accept the inevitable with good grace, our life will proceed quite smoothly and harmoniously."

—EPICTETUS

"Whenever you suffer pain, keep in mind that it's nothing to be ashamed of and that it can't degrade your guiding intelligence, nor keep it from acting rationally and for the common good. And in most cases, you should be helped by the saying of Epicurus, that pain is never unbearable or unending, so you remember these limits."

—MARCUS AURELIUS

"The happiness of your life depends upon the quality of your thoughts: therefore, guard accordingly, and take care that you entertain no notions unsuitable to virtue and reasonable nature."

—MARCUS AURELIUS

"As each day arises, welcome it as the very best day of all, and make it your own possession. We must seize what flees."

—SENECA

"He who is afraid of pain will sometimes also be afraid of some of the things that will happen in the world, and even this is impiety."

—MARCUS AURELIUS

"If you tell me that you desire a fig, I answer that there must be time. Let it first blossom, then bear fruit, then ripen."

—EPICTETUS

"Now is the time to get serious about living your ideals. How long can you afford to put off who you really want to be? Your nobler self cannot wait any longer. Put your principles into practice, now. Stop the excuses and the procrastination. This is your life! Decide to be extraordinary and do what you need to now."

—EPICTETUS

"If a man knows not which port he sails, no wind is favorable."

—SENECA

"What doesn't kill you makes you stronger."

—SENECA

"We should discipline ourselves in small things, and from there progress to things of greater value."

—EPICTETUS

"Choose whose life, conversation, and soul-expressing face have satisfied you; picture him always to yourself as your protector or your pattern. For we must indeed have someone according to whom we may regulate our characters; you can never straighten that which is crooked unless you use a ruler."

—SENECA

IV

WEALTH AS A TOOL

"Money is the least important thing that makes men free."

—Musonius Rufus

THE STOICS WEREN'T AGAINST money. They just refused to worship it. To them, wealth was like a sword, useful if handled well, deadly if it controls you.

Seneca was rich, but he wrote often about the trap of luxury. He warned that possessions easily become possessors. If money makes you cruel, anxious, or dishonest, then money is your master.

The Stoic way is simple: use money as a tool for purpose, to provide, to give, to build.

But never let it decide your worth. The only true master of your life is reason, virtue, and choice.

In Stoicism, money is viewed as something that can be useful but not essential for living a good and virtuous life. Stoic philosophers, such as Seneca and Epictetus, taught that wealth should never control your character or decisions. Instead, money should be used wisely with moderation and purpose to support basic needs, help others, and contribute to a stable life.

The Stoic approach encourages gratitude for what we have and warns against becoming attached to possessions or status. By treating money as a tool rather than as a measure of worth, a person can maintain inner freedom and remain focused on what truly matters: virtue, integrity, and living in accordance with nature.

"Receive wealth or prosperity without arrogance; and be ready to let it go."

—MARCUS AURELIUS

"The art of being a slave is to rule one's master."

—DIOGENES

"So, concerning the things we pursue, and for which we vigorously exert ourselves, we owe this consideration…either there is nothing useful in them, or most aren't useful. Some of them are superfluous, while others aren't worth that much. But we don't disarm this and see them as free, when they cost us dearly."

—SENECA

"Poverty is a virtue which one can teach oneself."

—DIOGENES

"The value of one's life is determined by how much love one gives, not by how much love one has received."

—EPICTETUS

"I have seen the beauty of good and the ugliness of evil."

—MARCUS AURELIUS

"Seek not the good in external things; seek it in yourselves."

—EPICTETUS

"What good are great possessions if their owner is enslaved by them?"

—MUSONIUS RUFUS

"No good thing renders its possessor happy, unless his mind is reconciled to the possibility of loss; nothing, however, is lost with less discomfort than that which, when lost, cannot be missed."

—SENECA

"The mind adapts and converts to its own purposes the obstacle to our acting. The Impediment to action advances action. What stands in the way becomes the way."

—MARCUS AURELIUS

"Wealth is not a good thing, nor is poverty a bad one."

—MUSONIUS RUFUS

"Drunkenness inflames and lays bare every vice, removing the reserve that acts as a chuck on impulses to wrong behavior."

—SENECA

"Remember, it is not enough to be hit or insulted to be harmed, you must believe that you are being harmed. If someone succeeds in provoking you, realize that your mind is complicit in the provocation. Take a moment before reacting, and you will find it is easier to maintain control."

—EPICTETUS

"It is better to be self-sufficient and live with less than to have much and depend on others."

—MUSONIUS RUFUS

"Pleasures when they go beyond a certain limit, are but punishments."

—SENECA

"We will train both soul and body when we accustom ourselves to cold, heat, thirst, hunger, scarcity of food, hardness of bed, abstaining from pleasures, and enduring pains."

—MUSONIUS RUFUS

"Some things are up to us and some things are not up to us. Our opinions are up to us, and our impulses, desires, aversions–in short, whatever is our own doing. Our bodies are not up to us, nor are our possessions, our reputations, or our public offices, or, that is, whatever is not our own doing."

—EPICTETUS

"So what you need is not those more radical remedies which we have now finished with, blocking yourself here, being angry with yourself there, threatening yourself sternly somewhere else, but the final treatment, confidence in yourself, and the belief that you are on the right path, and not led astray by the many tracks which cross yours of people who are hopelessly lost, though some are wandering not far from the truth path."

—SENECA

"When a dog is tied to a cart, if it wants to follow, it is pulled and follows, making its spontaneous act coincide with necessity. But if the dog does not follow, it will be compelled in any case. So it is with men to; even if they don't want to, they will be compelled to follow what is destined."

—ZENO OF CITIUM

"He who has equipped himself for the whole of life does not need to be advised concerning each separate thing, because he is now trained to meet his problem as a whole; for he knows not merely how he should live with his wife or his son, but how he should live aright."

—ARISTOTLE

"A stomach firmly under control, one that will put up with hard usage, marks a considerable step toward independence."

—SENECA

"First learn the meaning of what you say, and then speak."

—EPICTETUS

"If I followed the multitude, I should not have studied philosophy."

—CHRYSIPPUS

"No plague has cost the human race more dear: you will see slaughterings and poisonings, accusations and counter-accusations, sacking of cities, ruin of whole peoples, the persons of princes sold into slavery by auction, torches applied to roofs, and fires not merely confined within city-walls but making whole tracts of country glow with hostile flame."

—SENECA

"Dogs and philosophers do the greatest good and get the fewest rewards."

—DIOGENES

"A single day among the learned lasts longer than the longest life of the ignorant."

—POSIDONIUS

"How much better to heal than seek revenge from injury. Vengeance wastes a lot of time and exposes you to many more injuries than the first that sparked it. Anger always outlasts hurt. Best to take the opposite course."

—SENECA

"To be ignorant of what occurred before you were born is to remain always a child."

—CICERO

"As a matter of self-perseveration, a man needs good friends or ardent enemies, for the former instruct him and the latter take him to task."

—DIOGENES

V

STOIC VOICES ON WEALTH

"If you want to be rich, do not add to your money, but subtract from your desire."

—Epictetus

EPICTETUS BEGAN WITH NOTHING but a broken body and a sharp mind. He taught students that poverty could never touch a free spirit. Seneca sat in luxury yet battled restlessness. He urged readers to remember that wealth doesn't make you wise, it only amplifies who you already are.

Marcus Aurelius commanded armies, wealth, and power. Yet he scribbled in his journal: *"Do not value what is not your own."* An emperor writing to himself not to get lost in gold.

The voices are different, but the chorus is the same: wealth is external, fleeting, and indifferent. Your response to it is what matters.

Wealth may be useful, even preferable—especially when it allows you to live comfortably or help others—but it should never become a source of pride, attachment, or moral compromise. A Stoic understands that riches can be lost at any moment and therefore does not tie their sense of worth or peace to material possessions.

"Wealth is not to be measured by money, but by the number of things a man can afford to do without."

—EPICTETUS

"Thought is the fountain of speech."

—CHRYSIPPUS

"But money has been introduced by convention as a kind of substitute for need or demand. Its value is derived, not from nature, but from law and can be altered or abolished at will."

—ARISTOTLE

"We should every night call ourselves to an account: What infirmity have I mastered today? What passions opposed? What temptation resisted? What virtue acquired?"

—SENECA

"That it is our need which forms, as it were, a common bond to hold society together, is seen from the fact that people do not exchange unless they are in need of one another's services."

—ARISTOTLE

"You have power over your mind, not outside events. Realize this and you will find strength."

—MARCUS AURELIUS

"You can process in your intellect and senses a wealth of thoughts and impressions simultaneously."

—EPICTETUS

"Money is, indeed, subject to the same conditions as other things; its value is not always the same; but still it tends to be more constant than the value of anything else."

—ARISTOTLE

"I will begin to speak, when I have that to say which had not better be unsaid."

—CATO THE YOUNGER

"As you think, so you become...Our busy minds are forever jumping to conclusions, manufacturing and interpreting signs that aren't there."

—EPICTETUS

"The sea unites, rather than separates, the nations of mankind."

—POSIDONIUS

"Everything, then, must be assessed in money; for this enables men to always to exchange their services, and so makes society possible."

—ARISTOTLE

"In the constitution of the rational animal I see no virtue which is opposed to justice; but I see a virtue which is opposed to love of pleasure, and that is temperance."

—MARCUS AURELIUS

"Freedom is the only worthy goal in life. It is won by disregarding things that lie beyond our control."

—EPICTETUS

"Virtue is sufficient for happiness, but it is not indifferent to health, wealth, or strength, for these may be used in accord with nature."

—POSIDONIUS

"The acquisition of riches is not to be condemned, provided they do not lead us away from virtue."

—PANAETIUS

"No man was ever wise by chance."

—SENECA

"Receive [wealth or prosperity] without arrogance; and be ready to let it go."

—MARCUS AURELIUS

"The greatest good is a mind which despises chance and is content with virtue."

—POSIDONIUS

"I cannot escape death, but at least I can escape the fear of it."

—EPICTETUS

"Floods will rob us of one thing, fire of another. These are conditions of our existence which we cannot change. What we can do is adopt a noble spirit, such a spirit that befits a good person, so that we may bear up bravely under all that fortune sends us and bring our wills into tune with nature's."

—SENECA

"When someone is properly grounded in life, they shouldn't have to look outside themselves for approval."

—EPICTETUS

"Wealth should be acquired and used in ways that are honorable, never at the expense of justice."

—PANAETIUS

"The one is a philosopher without a tunic, and the other without a book: her is another half naked: Bread I have not, he says, and I abide by reason–And I do not get the means of living out of my learning, and I abide [by my reason]."

—MARCUS AURELIUS

"When you are offended at any man's fault, turn to yourself and study your own failings. Then you will forget your anger."

—EPICTETUS

"A man must so use his possessions that he is neither degraded by them nor too much exalted."

—PANAETIUS

"Any person capable of angering you becomes your master; he can anger you only when you permit yourself to be disturbed by him."

—EPICTETUS

"I don't at all condemn them in a spirit of malice, much less with an eye to seizing their property. I act in a spirit of concern and good will, like a doctor who comforts the patient whom he plans to cut open, and cajoles him into submitting to the operation."

—PACONIUS AGRIPPINUS

"The acquisition of riches has been for many men, not an end, but a change, of troubles."

—SENECA

"Seek not that the things which happen should happen as you wish; but wish the things which happen to be as they are, and you will have a tranquil flow of life."

—EPICTETUS

"If you follow reason, you will never miss the right path."

—CLEANTHES

"If you shape your life according to nature, you will never be poor; if according to people's opinions, you will never be rich."

—SENECA

"Education is the true wealth of life."

—POSIDONIUS

"Practice yourself, for heaven's sake, in little things; and then proceed to greater."

—EPICTETUS

"The Fates guide the willing, but drag the unwilling."

—CLEANTHES

"Circumstances don't make the man, they only reveal him to himself."

—EPICTETUS

"The universe itself is God and the universal outpouring of its soul; it is subject to this, and through this all things are bound together."

—POSIDONIUS

"The wise man is self-sufficient for happiness, for he needs only the strength of his own soul."

—CLEANTHES

VI

BUILDING RESILIENCE

"Never say of anything, 'I have lost it,' but, 'I have returned it.'"

—Epictetus

MONEY COMES. MONEY GOES. Fortune turns her wheel without asking your permission. The Stoics didn't brace against this, they prepared for it. They rehearsed loss in their minds so that when it came, it didn't crush them.

When wealth arrives, don't cling. When it departs, don't despair. Both are temporary. What endures is resilience, the ability to stand tall no matter what balance the ledger shows.

Every dollar you earn, every possession you hold, is only on loan. When it leaves, it returns to the universe. The only thing that remains yours is your virtue.

In Stoicism, wealth is seen as something temporary, always subject to change as fortune rises and falls. Philosophers like Seneca and Marcus Aurelius taught that money should be appreciated when it comes but never clung to, because it can disappear just as quickly as it arrived. The Stoics prepared themselves for this reality by reflecting on the possibility of loss, thereby strengthening their ability to remain steady when their circumstances changed.

From their perspective, every possession and every dollar is only temporarily entrusted to us, passing through our lives rather than belonging to us permanently. When wealth leaves, it simply returns to the world; what remains truly yours is your character.

"We need to envisage every possibility and to strengthen the spirit to deal with the things which may conceivably come about. Rehearse them in your mind: exile, torture, war, shipwreck. Misfortune may snatch you away from your country…If we do not be overwhelmed and struck numb by rare events as if they were unprecedented ones; fortune needs envisaging in a thoroughly comprehensive way."

—SENECA

"It takes a wise man to discover a wise man."

—DIOGENES

"Well-being is realized by small steps, but is truly no small thing."

—SENECA

"He needs little who desires but little."

—CLEANTHES

"We ought always to deal justly, not only with those who are just to us, but likewise to those who endeavor to injure us; and this, for fear lest by rendering them evil for evil, we should fall into the same vice."

—HIEROCLES

"The wise man is neither raised up by prosperity nor cast down by adversity; for always he has striven to rely predominantly on himself, and to derive all joy from himself."

—SENECA

"Remember that all we have is 'on loan' from fortune, which can reclaim it without permission, indeed, without even advance notice. Thus, we should love all our dear ones, but always with the thought that we have no promise that we may keep them forever, nay, no promise even that we may keep them for long."

—SENECA

"The Fates lead the willing, but drag the unwilling."

—CLEANTHES

"Associate with people who are likely to improve you."

—SENECA

"Living virtuously is equal to living in accordance with one's experience of the actual course of nature."

—CHRYSIPPUS

"Better to trip with the feet than with the tongue."

—ZENO OF CITIUM

"Life is very short and anxious for those who forget the past, neglect the present, and fear the future."

—SENECA

"He has his wish, whose wish can be to have what is enough."

—CLEANTHES

"He is a wise man who does not grieve for the things which he has not, but rejoices for those which he has."

—EPICTETUS

"True happiness is...to enjoy the present, without anxious dependence upon the future."

—SENECA

"Attach yourself to what is spiritually superior, regardless of what other people think or do. Hold to your true aspirations no matter what is going on around you."

—EPICTETUS

"If someone can prove me wrong and show me my mistake in any thought or action, I shall gladly change. I seek the truth, which never harmed anyone: the harm is to persist in one's own self-deception and ignorance."

—MARCUS AURELIUS

"Anger, if not restrained, is frequently more hurtful to us than the injury that provokes it."

—SENECA

"I have nothing to ask but that you would remove to the other side, that you may not, by intercepting the sunshine, take from me what you cannot give."

—DIOGENES

"You act like mortals in all that you fear, and like immortals in all that you desire."

—SENECA

"Everyone faces up more bravely to a thing for which he has long prepared himself, sufferings, even, being withstood if they have been trained for in advance. Those who are unprepared, on the other hand, are panic-stricken by the most insignificant happenings."

—SENECA

"Whenever you suffer pain, keep in mind that its nothing to be ashamed of and that it can't degrade your guiding intelligence, nor keep it from acting rationally and for the common good. And in most cases you should be helped by the saying of Epicurus, that pain is never unbearable or unending, so you can remember these limits and not add to them in your imagination. Remember too that many common annoyances are pain in disguise, such as sleepiness, fever and loss of appetite. When they start to get you down, tell yourself you are giving in to pain."

—MARCUS AURELIUS

"What is the point of dragging up sufferings that are over, of being miserable now, because you were miserable then?"

—SENECA

"He with the most who is content with the least."

—DIOGENES

"It does not matter what you bear, but how you bear it."

—SENECA

"The greatest wealth is a poverty of desires."

—SENECA

"Good luck betide! But it is the fifth hour now"

—PACONIUS AGRIPPINUS

VII

LIVING WEALTHY EVERY DAY

"Life is long if you know how to use it."
—Seneca

THE FINAL STEP IS practice. Wealth is not a theory, it's a discipline that you should live daily. Earn with integrity. Spend with purpose. Save without fear. Give without regret.

The Stoics invested in people more than possessions. They counted friendships, wisdom, and self-control as treasures no thief could steal.

Today, you can live Stoic wealth every morning when you wake up. Choose gratitude. Choose simplicity. Choose to measure your life by what you give, not what you stack.

That is the kind of wealth you cannot lose.

"For nowhere either with more quiet or more freedom from trouble does a man retire than into his own soul, particularly when he has within him such thoughts that by looking into them he is immediately in perfect tranquility."

—MARCUS AURELIUS

"He who fears death will never do anything worthy of a man who is alive."

—SENECA

"He who laughs at himself never runs out of things to laugh at."

—EPICTETUS

"In the constitution of the rational animal I see no virtue I see no virtue which is opposed to justice; but I see a virtue which is opposed to love of pleasure, and that is temperance."

—MARCUS AURELIUS

"The goal of life is living in agreement with nature."

—ZENO OF CITIUM

"This is our big mistake: to think we look forward to death. Most of death is already gone. Whatever time has passed is owned by death."

—SENECA

"Dwell on the beauty of life. Watch the stars, and see yourself running with them."

—MARCUS AURELIUS

"Money, then, as a standard, serves to reduce things to a common measure, so that equal amounts of each may be taken; for there would be no society if there were no exchange, and no exchange if there were no equality, and no equality if it were not possible to reduce things to a common measure."

—ARISTOTLE

"First say to yourself what you would be; and then do what you have to do."

—EPICTETUS

"Men do not care how nobly they live, but only for how long, although it is within the reach of every man to live nobly, but within no man's power to live long."

—SENECA

"Husband and wife should come together to craft a shared life, procreating children, seeing all things as shared between them, with nothing withheld or private to one another, not even their bodies."

—MUSONIUS RUFUS

"Let silence be your general rule; or say only what is necessary and in few words."

—EPICTETUS

"Time is like a river made up of the events which happen, and a violent stream; for as soon as a thing has been seen, it is carried away, and another comes in its place, and this will be carried away too."

—MARCUS AURELIUS

"Living comfortably to nature."

—SEXTUS

"Curb your desire—don't set your heart on so many things and you will get what you need."

—EPICTETUS

"When the light has been removed and my wife has fallen silent, aware of this habit that's now mine, I examine my entire day and go back over what I've done and said, hiding nothing my from myself, passing nothing by."

—SENECA

"To seek what is impossible is madness: and it is impossible that the bad should not do something of this kind."

—MARCUS AURELIUS

"Friendship always benefits; love sometimes injures."

—SENECA

"To refrain from fault-finding, and not in a reproachful way to chide those who uttered any barbarous or solecistic or strange-sounding expression."

—ALEXANDER THE GRAMMARIAN

"That's why the philosophers warn us not to be satisfied with mere learning, but to add practice and then training. For as time passes we forget what we learned and end up doing the opposite, and hold opinions the opposite of what we should."

—EPICTETUS

"Life is very short and anxious for those who forget the past, neglect the present, and fear the future."

—SENECA

"To do what was set before me without complaining."

—MAXIMUS

"Everything is only for a day, both that which remembers and that which is remembered."

—MARCUS AURELIUS

"Don't explain your philosophy. Embody it."

—EPICTETUS

"The happy man is satisfied with his present situation, no matter what it is, and eyes his fortune with contentment; the happy man is the one who permits reason to evaluate every condition of his existence."

—SENECA

"Let us be off and take our exercise."

—PACONIUS AGRIPPINUS

"If anyone tells you that a certain person speaks ill of you, do not make excuses about what is said of you but answer, 'He was ignorant of my other faults, else he would have not mentioned these alone.'"

—EPICTETUS

"Through the universal substance as through a furious torrent all bodies are carried, being by their nature united with and co-operating with the whole, as the parts of our body with one another. How many a Chrysippus, how many a Socrates, how many an Epictetus has time already swallowed up! And let the same thought occur to thee with reference to every man and thing."

—MARCUS AURELIUS

Final Thoughts

THE STOICS WERE CLEAR: money isn't the measure of a life well lived. It comes and goes, often without reason, and chasing it too hard can leave us emptier than before. Wealth can bring comfort, but it can also distract, corrupt, and control. What matters is how we choose to hold it…lightly, with perspective, never letting it hold us.

Zeno, Seneca, Epictetus, and Marcus Aurelius remind us again and again that real wealth isn't found in our bank accounts but in our mindset, our habits, and our character. Discipline over desire. Perspective over panic. Gratitude over greed. These are the true currencies of a free and steady life.

Everything external…money, possessions, even reputation…can be taken from us in a moment. But no one can strip away our integrity, our ability to respond with reason, or our commitment to live by our values. That's where the Stoics point us: toward a kind of wealth that isn't subject to fortune's rise and fall.

When we learn to treat money as a tool and not a master, we begin to experience what the Stoics called freedom. That freedom is the ultimate form of prosperity…and it's available to us right now, regardless of our net worth.

About the Authors

Nick Benas grew up in Guilford, Connecticut. A former United States Marine Sergeant and Iraq Combat Veteran, Nick is a 2nd Dan Black Belt in Tae Kwon-Do and a Green Belt Instructor in the Marine Corps Martial Arts Program. He holds an undergraduate degree in Sociology and an MS in Public Policy from Southern Connecticut State University. He has been featured for his business success and entrepreneurship by more than 50 major media outlets, including *Entrepreneur Magazine, Men's Health,* ABC, FOX, ESPN, and CNBC. His passion lies in serving veterans and writing.

Kortney Yasenka, LCMHC, is a licensed clinical mental health counselor who provides individual, family, and group therapy, as well as life coaching services. Kortney is certified in trauma-focused cognitive behavioral therapy and incorporates physical activity and eco-therapy into counseling and coaching sessions. She has a Masters in Counseling Psychology with a concentration in Health Psychology from

Northeastern University. With over 20 years of experience, Kortney has worked in community mental health, school systems, and private practice. In her free time, she enjoys running, spending time with family, and vacationing on the beautiful island of St. John.

Also by Nick Benas

Stoicism Quotes for Mind & Body
The Marcus Aurelius Book of Quotes
The Stoicism Book of Quotes
The Warrior's Book of Virtues
The Resilient Warrior
Warrior Wisdom
Tactical Mobility
Mental Health Emergencies

Also by Kortney Yasenka

Stoicism Quotes for Mind & Body
The Marcus Aurelius Book of Quotes
The Stoicism Book of Quotes
Swedish Lagom